Found in Trans

FOUND IN TRANSLATION

A hundred years of modern Hebrew poetry

Translated by
ROBERT FRIEND

Edited and Introduced by
GABRIEL LEVIN

MENARD PRESS
1999

Cover design by Charlotte Hodes

Worldwide distribution (except North America)
Central Books/Troika
99 Wallis Road, Hackney Wick, London E9 5LN
Telephone 0181 986 4854   *Fax* 0181 533 5821

Distribution in North America
Small Press Distribution Inc.
1341 Seventh Street, Berkeley, CA 94710, USA

ISBN 1 874320 23 3

Menard Press
8 The Oaks, Woodside Avenue
London N12 8AR, UK
Telephone and fax 0181 446 5571

Typeset by Antony Gray
Printed and bound in Great Britain by
Alden Press, Oxford

Contents

RACHEL

DAVID VOGEL

URI ZVI GREENBERG

ESTHER RAAB

YOCHEVED BAT-MIRIAM

HAYIM LENSKI

NATAN ALTERMAN

LEAH GOLDBERG

DAN PAGIS

NATAN ZACH

DAVID AVIDAN

DALIA RAVIKOVITCH

DALIA HERZ

ZALI GUREVITCH

With wine and fruit and flowers the table's laid.
But where's the guest whose spirit will be stayed?
The Host is lonely in the house He made.

YOSE BEN YOSE
(fourth/fifth century)

Introduction

Embarking upon his first, tentative translation of Hebrew poetry soon after arriving in Jerusalem in 1950, Robert Friend was in all probability quite unaware of just how far the journey would take him. He was in his mid-thirties, had published his first collection of verse in the United States in 1941, and before arriving in Israel had lived intermittently in Panama, Puerto Rico, France and Germany. Translating was obviously something he enjoyed, or at least felt to be an essential part of a poet's trade, as there are translations from the Spanish, French and German from this early period in his life. But at a deeper level translation was one way – and for a peripatetic poet perhaps the most vital way – of connecting to his adopted country and its poets.

Friend was characteristically modest in his approach to the task. Speaking of his versions of Leah Goldberg in an interview, he remarked, 'I thought of them as fun to do between writing my own poems. It had never occurred to me to publish them as a book until my friend Leah Goldberg died and I wanted to honour her in my own way.' That Friend's translations could sound at once natural and carefully attuned to the original, which the poet, with a limited Hebrew, was hearing only faintly, evoked among his friends a mixture of pleasure and astonishment: one couldn't help wanting to run to the original to tally the pros and cons of the English version, and translation is inevitably a delicate admixture of the two. Friend himself often remarked, half-seriously, that translating was not unlike setting out to solve the weekly crossword puzzle in the *New York Times*, of which he was a devotee.

A successful translation, however, is bound to transcend the mechanics of the crossword, so that in the final analysis we are left with what Friend called 'new flesh for the same spirit'. How this is achieved remains somewhat of a mystery, though a transfer of energy is clearly brought about by the translator's real or imagined relation to the original. Christopher Middleton has spoken of the work of translation 'as a kind of sensitive passion', a phrase that seems to me particularly applicable to Friend's own approach, which was at once playful and solicitous. Friend, as his name couldn't help implying, had always had a gift for friendship and more than anything else translation was a means of populating his basement apartment in the Jerusalem neighbourhood of Talbiyeh with the voices of other poets.

Thus the title of this selection – suggested by Friend shortly before he died – challenges Robert Frost's often quoted statement about poetry being 'what is lost in translation'. Translation, in Friend's case, enacted a process of discovery: what had been denied or distanced and muffled in the tangle of another language was now found, and made not only intelligible, but real and vitally *present*. Translation might offer, in short, moments of achieved closeness, even of intimacy, and one must remember that Friend lived, as an English-language poet, for close to fifty years in a culture and language that were never quite his own.

In some cases the bond was real. Leah Goldberg, Yehuda Amichai, Dan Pagis and Gabriel Preil were friends of the poet and the act of translating their work, over the years, deepened the ties. This was especially true for Goldberg and Amichai. The poet was, in fact, one of Amichai's first translators, and the translations presented here show a different, more formal, Amichai, than an English reader may be accustomed to. For Friend was always challenged by the formal pattern of a poem and taking on Amichai meant translating his sonnets, quatrains and couplets into their English equivalents. In Preil's case one witnesses the perfect match: an American in Israel, obdurately holding on to his expatriate status, translating the work of an Estonian-born Hebrew poet living a solitary, near-anonymous life in the Bronx. Then there were poets, like Natan Zach and Dalia Ravikovitch, who had attended Friend's classes on English and American literature in the budding, mid-fifties English department of the Hebrew University, temporarily housed in a building annexed to the King David Hotel in Jerusalem.

These were the living presences, who wrote in a limpid Hebrew that cut close to the contours of the spoken word. In the mid-sixties, however, Friend was invited to bring into English a large number of the early modern poets for an anthology published by the Institute for the Translation of Hebrew Literature. This was his first prolonged literary engagement with the originators of modern Hebrew poetry, beginning with Haim Nachman Bialik, revered by Hebrew readers and hailed as the country's first national poet, and extending to such poets as Yaakov Steinberg, Rachel, Uri Zvi Greenberg and Natan Alterman, to name only a few. The task was now considerably more difficult. Friend's Hebrew had always been shaky. He could manage a simple conversation and read, with some effort, the Hebrew paper. He had, I believe, just enough Hebrew to hear the tonal modulations of his contemporaries, such as Preil, Amichai, Goldberg and Pagis. But these were poets who had deliberately opted for a plain, pared down, conversational Hebrew that reflected, in essence, the 'latent music of its age', while the Hebrew of Bialik's generation and of the generation that followed, writing in Mandatory Palestine, was, if not quite foreign, altogether different.

Hebrew, its vocabulary and syntax, had evolved at breakneck speed, particularly during the first half of this century, and the truth of the matter is that for most native-born Israelis reading Bialik, Fichman and even the Whitmanesque Greenberg is not an easy task, to say the least, and requires prolonged study with a dictionary at hand. Friend was able partially to surmount this barrier by working closely with Hebrew scholars, notably Professor Shimon Sandbank, who would patiently and expertly guide the poet through the first drafts of a translation. Over the years Friend also developed his own approach, or practice of translation: the translator, Friend writes in his preface to his *Selected Poems of Ra'hel,* published in 1994, must take, at times, 'deliberate liberties'; he must, when necessary, substitute meters and rhyme schemes, tone down the diction and delete or add words, even an image or phrase, in order to create an equivalent 'incarnation' of the original. This is certainly close in spirit to contemporary theories of translation. Robert Lowell's *Imitations* and his admission to having been 'reckless with the literal meaning' in order to get the right tone also come to mind, though Friend's translations are certainly more cautious in their departures from the literal sense than Lowell's free versions.

If a problem arises it is when Friend is unable to hear or catch the tone of the original. Bialik posed such a problem for Friend, as he has for all of his translators into English so far. Perhaps it is a question of the music being lost in modern Hebrew, which is pronounced differently from Bialik's Ashkenazi Hebrew (in which the beat is always on the penultimate syllable). Friend would have had to negotiate between the old and new Hebrew in order to hear the exact imprint of Bialik's voice. Bialik himself nearly abandoned writing poetry once he settled in Tel Aviv in 1924, as if the cultural and linguistic gap between the diaspora and the new world was too great, even for the most eminent of poets. (He would, however, continue to write children's verse, sung in Israeli nursery schools to this day.) Friend returned to Bialik's verse once again in 1997, when he already knew that he did not have long to live. He translated close to a dozen poems, but admitted to not particularly liking Bialik, which might be another way of saying that he just couldn't hear properly its lyric strains. I have consequently included only those versions which do approach, to my mind, the original's elusive music – a policy that I have followed for all the poets presented here.

The wonder of Friend's translations is just how often he does manage to hear the complicated music of old-modern Hebrew verse. To hear, that is, and to reincarnate both its antique tone and its modern ring. I am thinking in particular of the 'decadent' poet and essayist Yaakov Steinberg, and of the lonely, Romantic figure of Rachel, of David Vogel, killed by the Nazis, of the fiery Revisionist, Uri Zvi Greenberg, and of the Russian Hebraist Hayim Lenski, who would write his last poems as he starved to death in Siberia. Here, a transfer of energy is immediately established. How does this happen? Perhaps it is a question of shared sensibilities, of hearing, almost preternaturally, the strains of a kindred soul. For the aforementioned are without exception poets of loss and displacement, for whom the Hebrew language becomes a locus for the intense interrogation of the self. 'The simple talk of my home', in Yocheved Bat-Miriam's words, would never really be a simple matter – a position that Friend knew all too well.

*   *   *

Whether translating to honour a friend, or out of a sensed kinship with a poet in the near-distant past, whether to earn one's daily bread, or out of a simple whim, the work accrued. Over several decades Friend published five volumes of translation (including a volume of children's verse by the Nobel Prize winner S. Y. Agnon, published posthumously). He also left a bulky folder of unpublished translations, mostly from Hebrew, but also including individual poems from Yiddish, German, French and Spanish, as well as a score of translations from Arabic, a language which Friend made repeated efforts to learn. In sifting through Friend's translations I found to my delight that the list of Hebrew poets was surprisingly close to being complete in its representation of the best of Hebrew poetry written in the last hundred years. There are of course poets that Friend never got around to translating, such as Amir Gilboa and Avoth Yeshurun, and of the generation who began publishing in the sixties, Israel Pincas,

Meir Wieseltier, Harold Schimmel, Yair Hurvitz and Yona Wollach. There are also, to my mind unsuccessful, or only partially successful, translations of a number of important poets which I chose not to include, such as Shaul Tchernikovsky, Avraham ben Yitzhak, Avraham Shlonsky and Yonatan Ratosh; and, of the younger generation, Aharon Shabtai and Mordechai Geldman. Friend's criteria for what constituted a felicitous translation were high, and I hope that in making my selection I have remained true the poet's own standards.

GABRIEL LEVIN

Acknowledgements

Grateful acknowledgment is due to the following publications where some of the translations were originally published: *Anthology of Modern Hebrew Poetry, Burning Air and a Clear Mind, The Burning Bush, Flowers of Perhaps: Selected Poems of Ra'hel, Focus, The Jerusalem Quarterly, The Jerusalem Post, Leah Goldberg: Selected Poems, The Literary Review, Micromegas, Midstream, Modern Poetry in Translation, Natan Alterman: Selected Poems, New Writing from the Middle East, P.E.N. Israel, Poetry, Sunset Possibilities and Other Poems, Voices from the Ark*. A version of the introduction appeared in *Modern Poetry in Translation*.

HAIM NACHMAN BIALIK

Only a single ray . . .

Only a single ray, but suddenly
you rise to glory and are half-divine;
one ray of sun unfolds the lure in thee,
unfolds the flesh. You ripen like a vine.

Only the tempest of a single night,
but it has ravished you of the sun's powers.
Already from afar, lewd dogs sniff out
the rotting corpse within the reek of flowers.

Summer night

True daughters of Lilith, night demons
weave and interweave with moonlight
gleaming silver threads, making one garment
for high priest and swineherd.

Once again a summer night begins,
houses empty, public gardens teem.
Once again, dreaming a giant dream,
men hasten to their little sins.

Impatient of spirit, in hope and desire blind,
'Stars,' they implore (it is all their prayer), 'be kind.
Shine nakedly in the heavens above, and show
the harlots shining nakedly below.'

In public gardens, stirring sleeping streams,
a thin, a winding music breaks the hush.
Under a tree a ribbon whitely gleams,
a shawl-fringe flashes darkly by a bush.

The golden stars tip winks like a bawd or whore
in calculation of a golden yield;
lust clings to every cobblestone and door
and to the sighing grasses of the field.

From river bank, from high balustrades,
from behind fences, murmurs and laughter float.
Naked arms reach up to lower shades,
and quick hot breaths blow the slow candles out.

And now at midnight, reeking of sweat and spunk,
down stairs, through alleys, the world's lovers, drunk,
stagger, or vomit, and through the vomit roll,
suffering in the flesh pollution of the soul.

True daughters of Lilith, night demons
weave and interweave with moonlight
gleaming silver threads, making one garment
for high priest and swineherd.

Stars shine and go out . . .

Stars shine and go out.
In the dark men decay.
Within my heart and everywhere
darkness holds sway.

Dreams sparkle and fade,
hearts flower and decay.
Ruins in my heart and everywhere
devour the day.

All pray for the light.
Lips rot as they pray.
This old, old tale long told, is told
again today.

How slowly, my friend,
night wears away.
Even the moon yawns wearily,
waiting for day.

If you found . . .

If you found my heart's scroll in the dust,
it would say:
he was weak and tired and simple,
but open as day.

Modest, he did what he had to,
working neither for praise nor blame,
accepting, without benison or curse,
whatever came.

A man who did what he had to,
not resisting his fate;
nor shied away from the petty,
nor aspired to the deeds of the great.

And when, uninvited, these came
on the king's highway,
the man simply stared in amaze at them,
then bowed and went away.

When the glorious knocked at his door,
he left it standing there,
loathing both the courage of dogs
and the righteousness of the hare.

The man had a little attic.
It was his alone.
There was no angel in it,
a devil there was unknown.

Overcome by sorrow,
he would climb its steep stairway,
and falling to his knees at the window
silently pray.

His was a life-long prayer,
but the Lord would not heed,
granting what he didn't ask for,
denying him what he did.

But the man kept on yearning for mercy,
and his heart would not despair
till it died as he was praying
in the middle of his prayer.

Summer is dying

Summer is dying in the purple and gold and russet
of the falling leaves of the wood,
and the sunset clouds are dying
in their own blood.

In the emptying public gardens
the last strollers break their walk
to lift their eyes and follow
the flight of the last stork.

The heart is orphaned. Soon
the cold rains will be drumming.
'Have you patched your coat for winter?
Stocked potatoes against its coming?'

At twilight

Come to the window
now that the sun is dying.
Wind your arms about me
till we blend into one.

So linked, we shall lift our gaze
to the terrible brilliance,
and release our thoughts
into that blazing sea,

and they in a bird-like rustle
of wings will soar
into the distant heavens
and be seen no more,

until, still flying,
they descend at last
on purple crags
and radiant islands.

Those are the distant islands,
the high worlds we saw in dream,
but they made strangers of us
and our lives a misery.

Those are the golden islands
that we longed for
as one longs for a homeland,
which all the stars of night

pointed to, led us to,
with trembling rays of light.
And we have been abandoned
on those islands,

with no companions, no friends –
two flowers of the wilderness,
two lost seeking a world lost
without end, without end.

My soul sinks

Under your love's burden
my soul sinks down, alas!
I, only a penny rattling
in your empty glass.

Why have you beset me?
What have I done wrong?
I, only a chopper of wood,
not a maker of song.

A woodcutter, a man of the axe,
working without complaining,
but the axe is blunted, the hand
hangs limp, the day is waning.

A hireling, I chanced on your woods,
looking for something to do –
in a time of no words for me,
no work for you.

How then shall we lift our faces?
How receive the morrow?
Let each take stock of his own world,
suffer each his sorrow.

Orphanhood

Strange was the way of my life – its paths were paths of wonder,
meeting between the gates of purity and defilement.
Holiness wallowed in blasphemy, piety in the unholy.
There, in a human swine cave, in the sacrilege of a tavern,
in fogs of incense, in steams of impious libation,
behind the spiced-wine barrels, over a yellow-leafed volume,
my father's head appeared, the skull of a tortured martyr.
It floated over his shoulders (as if beheaded) in smoke clouds,
his face sick with sorrow, eyes shedding blood.
Silent between his knees, I hung on his every word,
as the sots roistered about me, as the drunks sprawled in
                                                    their vomit.
The faces were monstrous, depraved, the words a filthy stream;
hearing, the walls made grimaces, the windows grew ashamed.
To a child's ear alone, a child still innocent,
the murmur of pure lips serenely, quietly flowed,
the murmur of Torah and Bible and the words of the living God.

Not long did I see my father, not long was my life with him.
When I was still young and tender, unsated with his look,
when my eyes still called for his mercy, my head for his
                                                    sheltering hand,
death came and took him from me, divided us forever;
but his image is deep in my heart: I call and he stands before me:
like an exhausted ox treading dumbly, slowly,
moving under its yoke, wide-shouldered, heavy of step,
steady and stiff and restrained, unchanged by time's changes
(dull days of sullen rain, dog days of feverish wind),
treading in gloom and dragging his life's crawling wagon
loaded with wearying stones on roadways heavy with mud,

FOUND IN TRANSLATION

on pathways of shifting sand, forever clouded with dust,
neck bent under the yoke, brow furrowed with worry,
eyes deep wells of grief, blankly, hopelessly staring
at every crossing of pathways, at every meeting of roads:
will there come from wherever he comes a merciful one,
                                        a redeemer?
So have I always seen him (and my soul grew dejected)
 – torn from God's lap in the morning, from the fountain
                                        of his life,
having doffed his garments of holiness, removed his *tefillin*
                                        and prayer-shawl,
when his eyes still beheld the soul, heart sang like a harp
                                        of wonder,
and his ears still heard the stars, still heard their distant
                                        murmur –
go out submissive and quiet like a somnambulist
to the suffering of his days and the sorrow of his hands:
he would sit his scorpion's day among stretched-out revellers,
drinking the steam of their mouths, defiled by the breath
                                        from their lips,
mounting the scaffold each day, thrown to the lions each day.
And when he returned in the evening, sweating with his disgrace,
drenched to the soul with disgust, as if from a pit of filth,
my heart for his suffering went out, I was smitten by his
                                        dumb grief.
If I had not been so young, if I had not been so weak,
I'd have put my neck to his neck, my shoulder to his shoulder,
bearing his burden with me, the yoke of his suffering.
If we had shared the burden, he might have found it lighter.
But wish exceeded reach, my prayers were all still-born.
He went his way as always, his lonely way of troubles,
soul bent to the ground with the burden and the effort,
and when they grew too much, his heart broke and he died.

In the middle of his days he fell down suddenly,
fell like a felled ox, down in the roadway
and never rose again.

   At the far end of the graveyard,
behind the slum of the tanners, the dwelling place of the poor,
among the graves of his brothers, the hungry, the
                              poverty-stricken,
laid like himself in the soil of death before their time,
washed clean of the dust of his world and cleansed of the
                              filth of his days,
in grave cloths white as his soul, white as the snows of morning,
wrapped in a shabby prayer-shawl, yellow as his books' pages,
pervaded like them with mercy, pervaded like them with prayer,
kissed by trembling lips and drenched with holy odours,
under a wooden grave mark of boards thin and hollow,
on a day of Elul, his bones at last found rest.
And over his head an inscription carved by no artist's hand
in faith attests: '*Hic jacet* a simple, honest man.'

Do not, although . . .

   Do not,
although he has exposed himself to you
   in utter nakedness,
bellow like bulls; he mocks you pitilessly
   and makes you pitiful.
You are too small for the meanings of his heart.
   He will reveal
not even the thousandth part

FOUND IN TRANSLATION

of what he thinks of you –
baring himself the better to conceal
   himself, to vanish from your eyes,
lead you astray.
   In the covert of his poems you search for him
in vain. They, too, conceal his secrets. But
   between the verses, as between the bars
of a steel cage, a sly, a burning lion peers,
   seemingly calm, resigned, or growling quietly –
a roaring fire shut up in his bones.
   One night, in the midst of your sweet sleep,
from a distance that you cannot guess,
   from a howling wilderness,
suddenly you will hear
   the echo of its thunder in dismay.
You will not understand.
   But a cage will have been broken, a lock
shattered, the lion escaped to his home.
   And in the morning of that night, at rise of sun,
magnificent, strong-hearted, he will stand
   atop a rock,
burning in his golden curls, ringed by his mane,
   everything about him crying King.
His nostrils will scent the quarry; his eyes flame
                              with scorn;
   his roar of freedom shiver the roots of the mountains.

LONDON 1931

᠁

YAAKOV FICHMAN

The Secrets of the Landscape

It is hardly enough to stir and mix
with a matching hand the pinks and the blues,
in effervescent colours fix
landscapes on canvas, all sorts of views.
What is scattered, gather; listen and remember;
arrest the moments before they flee;
a landscape captures the secret wonder,
the world's renewal in what you see.
False treasure like trash you must cast on the midden,
and the vain loveliness that led you astray;
rescue the little (that in hints hidden,
in the riddles of your dark blood kept from the day,
holds in its heart the secret, the glory).
One mastering stroke of your brush will lay bare
the world's dear things long lost and long buried.
Delve in that darkness and do not despair:
in that are *you*. The runes declare
the root of loveliness, the best of treasure.

Eve

I love Adam. He is brave of heart,
his blood is generous; and he, like God,
is wise. But the serpent whispers things
that are so strange. They hurt – and they caress.

When Adam sleeps, Eden lies desolate;
its birds are silent and its grass is wet.
And then *he* kindles, calling from the thicket,
a bonfire in my heart. 'Pick it! Pick it!'

How good to feel at dawn Adam's warm hand
caress my flesh again, and in the hush
listen to the coursing of its blood,
but every bush of day that drinks the light
bends to a darkness. Eden is enchanted
only till night awakes the shadow in the brush.

Jerusalem

Jerusalem! Cry of the hungry heart, oblivion's
garden beyond the hills when refugees fled the storm –
silence you are, submission and rebellion.
Because of you, heart shudders, the griefs swarm.

By green of your earth I swear and by your sunlight.
I inherit the desolation that remains.
I stand like a tree in stone, by you held spellbound –
soul woven with soul, my root in your dry veins.

I love what survives in you as in cold lava,
the rejoicing sound of ancient days,
echoing still from your white rocks of silence.

But with your holiness is now my strife,
and I have come to smash rocks into clods.
Dead splendour rests on furrows of new life.

YAAKOV STEINBERG

All of a summer

My small, my beautiful land, all of a summer
you sat beneath a canopy of blue;
the clinging sea defined your figure clearly
until the storm wind blew.

The storm wind blew; and now you showed your lovers,
as for a breath the blue line disappeared,
a face they had not known – its marvellous changes
born in a storm of tears.

Rain at night

In the heart of night, in winter, there was this hour:
suddenly down on the earth poured the strong rain –
and in its mouth the language of riddle and truth.

Magnificent rain of ever-increasing power,
with streams of an abundance never ending,
the many streams all blending in one song.

And when its plenitude approached past midnight,
night's secret boundary where sound no longer dwells,
the ultimate boundary of silence between yesterday and
tomorrow,

the rain grew troubled, flowing and rising in flood,
running its pure way from the living temple of heaven,
like a messenger from on high bringing the word of God.

Till evening

Whether to cry or whether to be proud,
I do not know. The change is very strange.
I hold less dear all worldly things, although
their forms become a thousand times more clear.

It is enchantment, deception, or a game,
and like a costly train grows ever longer.
The more my days increase, the more I note
the changes that life brings.

It is a vanity to guess and wonder
about the changeless end of every day:
things have become transparent and remote.
Their shadows move until the daylight fails.

FOUND IN TRANSLATION

It has been long . . .

It has been long since first my fears grew light.
My stubbornness in the ordeal cast off its dross,
the whole of my soul concealed death's nakedness.

Much has been shown me. Many can testify,
among good men and bad, that I
now kneel before the humble and the poor,
who once looked down at them from a proud height;

that I behold again the magic boundary
between those brothers: the future and happiness,
without lips' pride, without an armour for my nakedness.

I have striven long with many of the abashed
to find this refuge, where we need no longer fear
the weeping of our flesh, its hidden truth.

Turn towards the end . . .

Turn towards the end, be a leaf dying –
rottenness gilding it, the stem collapsing.
A faithful crimson gives regret beauty,
a humble withering hints the pride of every death.

Like original sin is the toil of all blooming –
beginning and ending; and life-lust makes muddy
will's every rebellion. Who, twisted or innocent,
ought to disdain then what poverty offers,
and go towards his rest in the yoke of complaining?

Poor, blind the solution; but as the best man,
                          the bridegroom,
meekness and solace silently lead him,
and they walk securely on the sad pathway,
beholding all clearly to life's last boundary.

RACHEL

Love was late in coming . . .

Love was late in coming, and coming
didn't dare call out: I am here,
while she knocked on the doors of the heart,
and stood as a poor man stands,
hands silently stretched out.
Her look was sad and imploring,
submissive and filled with doubt.

Pale are the candles, therefore,
that I have lit for her,
pale as the last flowers
in the autumn light;
hesitant my joy, therefore,
quiet and in pain
like the pain of hope disappointed,
or waiting, waiting in vain.

He too will soon go away . . .

He too will soon go away
without a goodbye.
So his sad eyes say
and the bitterness that lingers
at the corners of his mouth.
Gravely he watches
children at their play,
or rages, and then grows suddenly still,
as if to say,
Nothing matters and nothing ever will.

We shall find him gone one night
from his place among his friends,
and suddenly pale with fright,
and a certainty of doom,
we shall all of us rush to his room.
He will not be there.
Only his last letter on a table,
staring blankly white.

In my great loneliness . . .

In my great loneliness
of a wounded animal,
I lie for hours and hours. Lie silent.
Fate has harvested my vineyard, not even sparing
the young grapes.
But the humble heart has forgiven.

If these days are my last days,
I shall be quiet
lest my defiance sully
the peaceful blue of the sky,
My longtime friend.

Surrender

He is breathing his last, my rebellion is dying –
that fiery, proud, and gay one.
Surrender, a pale widow,
approaches my house in silence.

She pries my clenched teeth open,
loosens my fists closed tightly.
She fetches ashes in handfuls
to cover the last of my embers;

and with head bowed down and silent
creeps into a distant corner.
I know too well she will never
leave my house again.

Tiny joys . . .

Tiny joys, joys like a lizard's tail:
a sudden sea between two city buildings in the west,
windows glittering in the setting sun –
everything blessed!

Everything blessed.
A consoling music in everything,
in everything mysteries and hints –
and everything waiting for corals of beautiful words
to be strung by the imagination on its string.

Wrestling

Alas! When the instinct rules,
my helpless hands are drawn
to the glamour of ruby and pearl,
to words as beautiful
as any precious stone.

They know its power is great.
What it plans they carry out.
It blinds with a shower of light,
makes deaf with a golden sound.

I cannot see the dawn
or hear the silences.
Was it I who swore faith to words
as simple as a shout?

The barn

We used to sleep, you remember,
on top of a heap of wheat.
The shame when the first rays woke us
as they smiled through a pitchfork's teeth.

And as we slept, you remember,
all the streams of light
that watered the fields of the homeland
poured through us in the night.

And as they poured, they blessed us,
renewed us and fulfilled us.

That light is with me still.

At the window

There is something after all of pleasure
in this sad world of ours:
in the small courtyard below, my neighbour's
garden of greens and flowers:

Two furrows of curling pea tendrils
aspiring towards the skies,
of onions over-cheeky
and radish with red eyes.

From the furrow below a figure
forgotten and loved in vain
climbs towards a high window
and peers silently through the pane.

The messenger came in the night . . .

The messenger came in the night
and sat on my bed,
his body all protruding bones,
the eye-holes deep in his head;

and I knew time's hands were dangling
(as though the words were unspoken),
that the bridge between future and past
had broken.

A bony fist now threatened,
and I heard aghast
sardonic laughter that said:
'This poem will be your last.'

My dead

Only the dead don't die

Only they are left me, they are faithful still
whom death's sharpest knife can no longer kill.

At the turn of the highway, at the close of day
they silently surround me, they quietly go my way.

A true pact is ours, a tie time cannot dissever.
Only what I have lost is what I possess forever.

DAVID VOGEL

With gentle fingers . . .

With gentle fingers
the rain is playing
a secret, sorrowful melody
on the black piano of night.

Now in the dark we sit
each in his home
– the children have fallen asleep –
listening to the rain
because it tells of our sadness.

Our mouths no longer have the words;
our feet are weary
with the day;
no dance in them any more.

On autumn nights . . .

On autumn nights
a leaf falls in the woods unseen,
lies silently on the ground.

A fish leaps from the waters
of a stream,
and in the dark
a flapping wetness echoes.

In the black distance are sown
hoofbeats of horses unseen,
dissolving.

All this
the weary wanderer hears
and trembles in his bones.

Silently you stand before me . . .

Silently you stand before me,
your azure gaze
passes me sadly,
floats towards the horizon.

Where are you sending your soul?
Not yet do your longings
flutter around me
like brilliant butterflies.

A wanderer now, you are going from me.
But your crooked staff
will guide you.

And when your feet are treading the far wood
your quiet footsteps
in my yearning soul
will rustle silently.
Rustle endlessly.

Waiting-rooms

Heavy curtains in the waiting rooms
of famous doctors drape the windows like a pall;
no distant murmur of men ascends to them,
no rattle of wagons from the streets below.

Around the room pictures of long ago
gaze darkly; statues freeze before they spring.
Deep is the red of cupboard and of wall;
an ancient silence covers everything.

A man drowns in these heavy silences,
lost in the chair's upholstery, a light put out,
an object like the objects all about.

But when on the softness of rugs a step draws near,
a shiver goes through him, shakes him out of his ease.
He stares at the doctor with great bulging eyes.

A single and last carriage . . .

A single and last carriage is ready for the journey.
Let us get in –
it will not wait.

I have seen timid girls depart –
their narrow faces
flushed and mournful
like scarlet sunsets;

and round and rosy children
innocently ride off
simply because they were called.

And I've seen men
who walked the streets of the world
proud and erect,
their large eyes piercing far
from where they stood –
they too got into the carriage leisurely
and drove off.

We are the last.
The day is ending
and one last carriage is ready for the journey.
Let us step into it quietly and start –
we, too –
because it will not wait.

URI ZVI GREENBERG

Song of the great mind

That mind – the small one – is soft, like a pullet;
it is afraid of space and it loathes the dimensions of the sea;
it is a forest firefly at night,
a tavern's splinter of light in the meadow-night
to the eyes of the carter
as sluggishly he drives horse and cart
through the dust, and yawns.
Such is the mind – the small, the poor one – that serves
the peddler on his daily rounds;
and that twistedly scorns visions of glory.
It goes through our streets near the low roofs,
licking the moss of days, drinking from drainpipes,
seeing in every cur a kind of wolf or tiger.

That mind – the great one, the one winged with light,
the supreme ruler, the high king
(from the time the people inhabited their lands and waters,
and the king from his throne
beheld the mountains of Moab) –
is not here. It sits in its nest forgotten,
but it lives. I sing to my people: remember the eagle!
Bid it come, and it will come,
to show you

the place of passage that leads from here, the swamp of dream . . .
to the meaning.

So poor are we without, so twisted of shape, so shorn of glory;
not so within the body, which is more deep
than its bodily dimensions. In it hidden lie
as in a locked palace
all kinds of marvellous and precious things,
until the tall and wide gate of the heart
is broken through by the gate-breaker
blowing a ram's horn.

Towards that day I sing; and in the hearts
of our generation, in every song,
I stir up the strife of longing. My every syllable cuts.
I catch each traitor, though disguised. I strip him bare
who teaches us to be as a reed to the river.

So poor without, such mighty lords within!
Mighty like the mountains of Lebanon,
eternal like Mount Hermon in its snows.
And that sundering in the middle? Amen, I sing the day
on which the miraculous line of the race which Titus rent in two
will be joined.

I thirst for water . . .

I thirst for water; wine is my need no longer,
opium no longer.
Let my brain be clear till I am that I am.
My equator – in consciousness of being.

I neighed like a colt in the sun. And joy,
even at my sandal's tip, invaded me,
brimmed at my footsteps.
Now I know: joy ever came to me
not to subtract from sorrow, but to destroy.

Now like a child I keep watch at the mirror, and see
someone there who watches me, so much resembling me.

Song of earth

We shall not lift our eyes towards the heavens –
we are not the sons of the giants nor their daughters.
Who imprinted, like a seal, on our soul this fruitless sky-yearning?
In truth, we are like trees whose roots are here . . . our fate is theirs:
in the joy of blossoming, the giving of fruit, in being a stump;
                                                    and in their death
at the woodcutter's hand . . . As they are in the secret of the forest,
                                    we are in the secret of the people.

We no longer have anything in heaven . . . there a face is
                                                turned away –
in so much blue, so many clouds.

URI ZVI GREENBERG   31

All that is lost, all that still exists in its truth, its grace, its
needle-like pain,
exists here in the lower world:
here our mother conceived us, and here our father
ate the first apple;
here we milked the first goats, the baker erected his house
near the grain of the sun.
How good the bread tasted then.
Soon in this circle of bread, we, man and woman,
shall seal our life's kingdom.

Here we poured our good words, casting them into best thoughts,
myrrh and wine in a thousand songs for the blossoming of love,
here from a neighbouring, lowly rock we struck a spark of fire,
and here we raised the banners of rebellion.
Let us turn our eyes to the earth, to the mirrors of rivers and seas,
where our lost ones lie hidden, the warm ones dear to the heart,
dear to the soul.

Here, too, lies hidden our strength's sword; and here it hacked
to pieces
the enemy; and piece by piece we'll gather them because
in gathering there is a blessing.
And we shall cast into the melting pot
the pieces; like David, forge a sword with which to forge
a covenant with the peoples
who live by sword and spade and song.
Who seeks to destroy our blood, we shall slay him with a sword.

Here, here below are the dear, the holy, the lovely –
all the lost, for whom we shall yearn and grieve and even die.

.

The hour is tired . . .

The hour is tired as if it were time for bed;
and like a foundling in a white nightshirt only,
I sit and write in the void as if upon a blackboard:
nothing matters, nothing matters.

If the black cat should leap among the platters, lap up
what's left of the white milk, and overturn the platters,
I'd close my eyes for sleep, I'd sleep forever –
nothing matters, nothing matters.

Song to heaven

Heed us when we turn our eyes to heaven
in a time of yearning, a time of sorrow,
when our yearning rises in song:
as if our daughters and we were descendants of the giants.
Once our crown was made of the sun's gold,
and our garments, once, of moon stuff.
Mothers prepared our beds on carpets of azure
in star brightness . . . our childhood ages ago.
And still today we have no space for blossoming,
in which to eat our life's fruit, drink its waters
and grind, in hard-toothed fury, our fetters into dust.
We see in our shadow's tremor the secret of our ruin.
Not the language of the lowlands is the language
of our heart, our soul, our blood;
and we breathe – alive – not the air of this present, but

– above the tree-tops of the usual and all the mountain
                                        peaks of dailiness –
the air of our ancient days.
For in our depths there lives the song of the heavenly ones,
our shoulders tell the secret of the clipping of our wings.

Our richest resemble in this our poorest poor . . .
I cannot distinguish between them. I have not my life long,
neither on sea or land, for our bodies
are given to sorrow and to longing,
given to weeping, and our weeping ascends to heaven.
Having vowed to remember the heavenly ones, we shall
                                        not break this vow
until the saviour comes, to lead us
back to our ancient greatness.

I have never been . . .

I have never been at the top of wind-played Olympus.
I grew up with bread in the valley of living man.
Like every man I drank from the good waters of the valley,
from the waters lapped by the cattle whose flesh I ate.

My fathers bore no queen's train among the alien nations.
No emperor called for them either in joy or grief.
They were Jews – poor and shining and singing
what the poor shepherd pipes upon his flute –

It is good, therefore, to take myself from pain to pain
as the shepherd takes his sheep from pasture to pasture,
living on dried figs.

Red are the fringes of day, the ends of the night.

Song of my people-forest, people-sea

When a man walks in the forest and lifts his voice there,
the great forest answers with an echo-echo,
a sign that the voice has entered and shaken its forest heart;
but when a man wanders the sea and lifts his voice to the sea,
the sea never answers, the water goes on flowing . . .
Like the voice of a man on the open sea, such is the voice of
                                                    the seer
in my people-that-are-a-sea . . . my people-sea! In the
                                        manifold world.

But my people-sea, who are a sea for all their seers,
are a forest everlasting for the peoples of the world:
giving the best of wood for pillars and sills
and roofs of palaces;
cloud after cloud will be sent on the head of my people-forest
to the alien nations; they will come
to lay the trees low. There the beasts of prey assemble.
When an alien people rise beyond my forest-people and lift
                                                their voices,
my people-forest will answer them!
Not so when a prophet and seer with powerful voice stands up
                                        from within them,
and where he stands, there is the heart of the sea . . . my
                                                people-sea!

In truth, a curse of generations, a sin of generations . . .
a sadness not even madness can overcome!
Is it of God, this cruelty?

Happy the innocent or fool, happy the man, ignorant of the
                                        heart of this,
like the blind and deaf harper when his hands are on the strings,
like the man who walks, led by imagination's miracle,
behind a plough in the heart of the sea,
and thinks: a field! And ploughs furrows in the waters;
a field! And casts seed upon the waters . . .
But woe unto the seer-sage who knows the secret,
a fear in his luminous mind
until his mind trembles, a torch in the wind . . .

He knows that this is a sea and not a field
but walks on the sea and ploughs and sows:
perhaps a miracle will happen; and the cruel god

of generations, leading a desert wind, will bid the sea to be
                                        a continent;
the sea and the waves of the sea turn field and its fat furrows,
and that which was sown in it in the knowledge of a
                              longed-for miracle
rise green and golden,
every grass according to its kind, every tree, and all the grains
                                        of the sun.

All my days and all my nights are a prayer for the miracle.

URI ZVI GREENBERG   37

&

ESTHER RAAB

A serenade for two poplars

Tonight I have a date
with two tall poplars
and a tall palm.
Man's dwellings beneath
murmur like beehives,
are cosy, are warm.
But I –
I feel good tonight
with two poplars
and a tall palm –
light clouds in their branches,
quince fragrance in hedges,
shadows on asphalt.

Folk tune

The great tiger
loved me –
and I loved him.
He had eyes
of an extinguished blue
with the skin sagging about them:
wrinkles, wrinkles . . .

I searched among the wrinkles
for the blue of his eyes
as for cold water
hidden in mist.
He smelled like a forest,
smelled like a hunter:
a hunter whose quarry
was wild beasts and women.
He lived beyond time.
He was
'the eternal tiger' –
granter of visions,
dispenser of dreams,
collector of pain.

Today I am modest . . .

Today I am modest like an animal,
open like rain-drenched fields.
With a little fat hand I guide my life
toward compassion and children.
Every stranger, every sufferer
comes to me today.
The little gifts of my heart
patter about me like rain.
And I am already carrying Tomorrow –
a heaviness
closed
and leaping again
toward the unknown.

YOCHEVED BAT-MIRIAM

The monasteries lift gold domes . . .

The monasteries lift gold domes,
crosses, crosses. I weary, seeing them.
I speak in parables and they are strange;
otherwise, I could not meditate.

The memory of the ancient generations
rises like a vision: a temple strong and splendid.
The roads are humming like encircling rivers,
an exultant throng draws near.

We have fled, today, the parables of Mount Hermon,
of Mount Gilboa and the fields of Carmel;
Sharon and Galilee mourn only in the adage,
the lordly cedar only in the proverb.

Left with my poverty, I envy
every sown valley rising like a song.
An exile, strange to every wind,
may I be given field and fallow land.

Oh may my home be like a kneeling camel,
my days move onward like yoked mules;
my silent soul howls like the jackals,
and cries out like the sea!

Precious stones . . .

Precious stones that my mother
hid when no one was by,
each shone next to each other,
strung by prayer and sigh.

Two knots in her kerchief were
her secret signallings.
For me its white ends moved
like a bird with hidden wings.

Tender, compassionate,
she went by silently;
the memory falls on my heart
of her shining humility.

Her eyes bright with tears,
I kneel before my daughter,
and my mother's precious stones
appear in the shining water.

The sound of the waves in the silence . . .

The sound of the waves in the silence
on the boundary of the fading and dim,
the distant and dying splendour –
what is it hinting of?

My daily path lies before me
as if it continued the sky.
In my dwelling, when I come to my dwelling,
I shall find the miraculous star.

I shall close my eyes of longing
to see the impossible worlds;
the din of their flight in the heavens
will pour chaos and cloud.

Until I have comprehended
the dust at my feet in white
with the sand of their path that stretches
as a sign from afar, a command.

Until I have comprehended
the simple talk of my home
is but the talk that traverses
from star to star – to the earth.

Without a boundary or threshold,
as tree to tree in the shade –
this world to the world we have longed for –
my talk with the talk of God.

YOCHEVED BAT-MIRIAM

43

❦

HAYIM LENSKI

Wormwood has enchanted me . . .

Wormwood has enchanted me completely,
with bitterness of juices sharply smelling.
For wormwood's sake and only for its sake,
I wander, Cain, a man without a dwelling;
a shoot of wandering, by the east-wind beaten,
and for no sin, stoned by the sharp-edged hail.
Its hair of greenish-white is more compelling,
is dearer to me than the red of roses,
or even your lips' red, O Beauty's daughter.
No, do not mock me with your laughter.
I'm not a saint. I'm not an anchorite –
wormwood has enchanted me completely.

Day turns to evening . . .

Day turns to evening on the lake.
The fish descend to sleep and the wave hushes.
Birds cease their chatter in the brake.
How melancholy are the rustling rushes!

The echo of what voice complains?
The echo of whose voice where the reeds sway?
The shore is desolate. No foot has trod these plains
since the world's first day.

Of longings that have found no words,
of days whose sun set long ago,
of the migrations of the birds –
the rushes whisper to the lake below.

Lightly a slight shadow . . .

Lightly a slight shadow floats on the March snows.
Look! A starling is making its swift flight.
The horizon is pierced by its bill. A chick
from the crack of eggshell-thinness pecks its way.

Another day! Another day!
The stream bursts through its carapace of ice,
and the first thunder
shatters the silence of fields.
To their old nests birds return with a song.
My land, I shall see thee, I will see thee yet.

Incredible spendour . . .

Incredible spendour – ethereal, delicate!
What transparency!
With one slight breath drawn from the deep breast,
the pattern that we know ceases to be.

Uprooted, everything is flying.
No wonder that a leaf – a leaf? – a tree is soaring.
There is no miracle, and not one thing is hidden.
Everything's revealed. The tree, the whole tree's soaring.

You raise your voice – no echo; you bend your
                                         head – no shadow.
You are lighter than the webs of late September.
Matter shakes off the burden of its weight
as riffling a book's pages frees it of its words.

Light, my light . . .

Light, my light, who commanded, 'Disappear!'
November world, world in darkness now.
The scythe lies silent in the field,
the roof-straw's drenched
with the last after-holiday rains.

And I have a letter to finish. The blotter is heavy.
There's nothing to say. And what can I invent?
Dear God!
The mouth yawns, the hand writes:
'Send Uncle my regards.'

The moon's brightness . . .

The moon's brightness turns a freezing blue;
she trembles as if taken by a fever.
An hour will pass, a second, or a third –
and the storm will break forth in anger.

Over land and island, over the sea
her majesty the storm will soon be sweeping.
Armed with the lightning, to the beat of the thunder's drum,
cloud legions will come streaming.

Our generation's ruled by the house of Mars,
and the hand of fate cannot be stayed, my brother.
I know this well, since drunk with insanity's wine,
we kill each other.

And yet the storm will end, a rain will fall,
a quiet meadow wind stir into being,
and over a dead tree trunk, a waking bluebell
with tongue of dew will carol in the morning.

Near the mill

Clattering hoofs of horses, glitter of metal.
Hetman to Cossacks said:
'The miller's a kite!' And they leaped from the saddle.
Black were the boots that entered the mill;
the boots that left were red.

Clattering hoofs of horses, glitter of metal.
Said a Red-Army lad: 'For a lark,
I'll look in on my dad.' And he leaped from the saddle.
Bright was the day when he entered the mill,
and when he left, it was dark.

Clattering hoofs of horses, glitter of metal.
And the soldier turned him back
to his camp and his flag. And a fall wind scattered
the flour from his coat, the flour from his hair
that will never again be black.

There broke into my cell . . .

There broke into my cell last night
a whistle from the train of winds.
Though I was half asleep, feet leaped ahead.
'Forward, while strength remains!'

Forward! And in a flash I stood
upon a train step, at a door.
Nobody asked, 'Where from?' Nor I,
'Where are you headed for?'

Darkness flowed like streams of tar
round about my window pane
as shawls of snow from the north pole waved
goodbye to the departing train.

South to the homeland! But who had changed
the window to a drum and hit it?
A finger at the Judas-window rapped:
'Hiding beneath the covers not permitted.'

NATAN ALTERMAN

Summer night

Silence whistles in the open spaces.
A knife in cat's eye glows.
Night. How much night! In the sky, stillness.
Stars in swaddling clothes.

A wide, wide time. The heart's clock strikes two thousand.
Dew, like a rendezvous, veils the eyelashes.
A streetlamp hurls black slaves across the pavement
as its gold whip flashes.

A summer wind wanders, dim and agitated,
lips tonguing the shoulders of the gardens.
A greenish evil. Suspicions, lights – fermenting.
A treasure seething under the froth of darkness.

And high on the mountain, with a famished roaring,
its eyes a golden fire,
wrathfully a city vaporises
amidst stone pillars, and soaring dome and spire.

Moon

Even an old landscape has a moment of birth.
The birdless heavens
are impregnable and strange.
Moonlit, under your window, lies your city
bathed in cricket-weeping.

But when you see that the path
still looks at the wanderer,
and that the moon
rests on a spear of cypress,
you ask in wonder: 'Are all of these still here?
Can I still whisper my greetings to them?'

The waters gaze at us from their lagoons.
The tree in its red of earrings keeps its silence.
Never, my God, shall the sadness of Your huge playthings
be uprooted from me.

First smile

Do not call me with many words. Do not call me with
                                                    desperate vows.
    I am gathered to you again.
From all my weary paths I climb to your threshold now.
    Do not call me with many words.
Everything shrivels and rots. But you and the night still live.
So many things wait their turn at the threshold of the heart,
stand with fist extended, in an unruly queue –
    and the night, the night still lives.
Its darkness smokes from chimneys, its forest rage.
    And it uncages tumult like a zoo.

If yet your eyes remain, mourning in their sleepless rings,
or your name that made a music with its triple strings,
now covered with dust, and shut, no longer a source of song –
tell that old sorrow of yours, tell the silences
that murder tears: one always returns to them,
    returns with an empty heart
from blazing brand and torch, from smoking towns of war,
to embrace – if only once – to embrace them once more.

    Momentous the moments of the end!
Snuff the candles out. The light cries out for rest.
Enfold me in your silence. Distances are adrift.
And I am breathing air at a raving altitude.
    You! Never have I lived
in you! You are my sea, salt savour of my land!
Yes sometimes your memory will seize me suddenly,
with a tiger's hungry leap, with winds and flying doors,
with a tempestuous joy, with broken-winged happiness.

NATAN ALTERMAN

Somewhere in shadow, I know, you wait for me, a shade
with bitten, trembling lips. I have heard your whisper swoon,
catch up with the horses, hide in shed or stable.
How often amid the fumes of a lonely feast, my head
dying on a table, I have seen you in some nook,
when all the guests were gone, standing in the gloom
   to freeze me with cold hands.

For the swift, the silent years have gone past your door,
for in their little casket, your earrings lie dead,
for a leanness, cold and sure, has carved your face and head.
And when you come toward me, like a stumbling ghost, and stand
against a far horizon that shrouds with cloud the blaze,
you preserve for me what is most precious to me,
and redeems all my days: a dry crust of sorrow,
the light of a first smile – that crumbles to dust.

The Mole

Not in vain I vow to be faithful,
not in vain I tag at your heels.
With the Mole I struggled from darkness,
stubborn and under a spell.

You, grief of the nails on my fingers,
you, woe of my head growing bald,
hearing me in the cracking of plaster,
in the spreading silence of mold.

In a mirror inlaid with copper
your humble candle sways.
Those who go toward your face in the darkness
have watched from their hiding-place.

But when I stole forth to steal you,
your candle blinded me.
Bristling and dark before it
remained the Mole and I.

*

Not in vain did I vow to be faithful.
Assaulting the earth where I dwell,
I longed toward your life from my darkness,
for life casts spell upon spell.

See me absurd, my wonder!
Rehearsing you clue by clue,
the way you stand, your gestures.
And trembling with you for you.

My every thought besieged you –
the hairs of my head upright
as I thought of bread on the table
and the candle shedding its light.

Bent and old like your mother,
I held you to my breast,
bearing your misery for you
without refuge from you or rest.

You – grief of the nails on my fingers,
you – woe of my balding head,
burden of my midnight brooding,
burden I cannot forget.

Because our foes persevere,
and you break like a stalk of grain,
bristling and dark before them
only Mole and I remain.

In a mirror inlaid with copper
see the candle flicker and spark.
Never shall we forget you,
our faces say from the dark.

For the world is riven, and double
the clamour of its distress.
For no dead have forgotten their dwellings,
all dwellings mourn somebody dead.

At our cities of sorrow forever
gaze the dwellers of darkness and mound.
The glory of our days brims over
with thought of the dead underground.

The spinner

Silent the girl at the spindle
spun a scarlet thread.
She has spun me a royal mantle,
a king in his throne-room said.

Silent the girl at the spindle
spun a black midnight thread.
She has spun me a robe for the scaffold,
a thief in his dungeon said.

Silent the girl at the spindle
spun a golden thread.
She has spun me a garment to play in,
a wandering mummer said.

Silent the girl at the spindle
spun an old grey thread.
She has spun us a coat to mourn in,
a beggar and his mongrel said.

She took all the threads from the spindle
for the last robe she would spin.
Then down she went to the river
and washed her pure white skin.

And she put on the robe of her weaving –
no brighter ever was seen.
And now she is thief and beggar,
and she is mummer and queen.

The shadow

There was a man and his shadow.
And standing up one night, the shadow took
his master's coat and shoes,
put on the shoes, got dressed.
Crossing the room, he took
his master's hat from off a hook,
tried to take off his master's head as well.
In vain.
He took the face instead,
and before you could say boo had clapped it on.
He left the house in the morning with a cane.

His master pursued him down the street,
yelling to those who knew him as he ran:
'Terrible! Terrible!
That thing's a shadow! A charlatan! – not a man.
It certainly isn't me!
I'll write to the government.
He won't get away with this. He'll see.'
But little by little he got used to it,
and he calmed down.
In the end he forgot the entire incident.

The householder departs from the city

Going to his room one night,
he locked his door and by lamplight
counted his money, counted his foes.
Then from the table of his heart
he struck off every name but one,
which would be there till time was done.
Then rising, he turned off the light.
Sprouting feathers, wings, and bill,
he hopped on to the window sill,
and sailed, a bird, into the night.

❧

LEAH GOLDBERG

Tel Aviv 1935

The roof-poles in those days
were like the masts of Columbus,
every crow on their pinnacles
announcing new shores.

Along the streets strolled knapsacks,
and the words of a foreign country
plunged into *khamsin* days
like the cold blade of a knife.

How could the small air support
so many recollections
of childhood and of withered loves
and rooms grown empty elsewhere?

Like blackening snaps in a camera,
their images reversed:
white winter nights across the sea,
rainy nights of summer,
capitals dark at dawn.

Behind you foreign footsteps drummed
the marching songs of an army,
and on the sea you thought you saw
the church of your old town floating.

In the Jerusalem Hills

1

I lie like a stone on the hill,
indifferent and silent
in the withered, sun-seared grass.
Pale skies touch rock.
Where does the yellow-winged butterfly
come from?
A stone among stones, I do not know
the ancientness of my life
or who will yet come
and with a kick
send me rolling down the slope.

Perhaps it is beauty frozen forever,
perhaps eternity
moving slowly.
Perhaps it is
a dream of death,
or a dream
of the one love.

I lie like a stone on the hill
in thorn and thistle,
where a road below slides to the city.
Soon the wind that blesses all things
will come, to caress the pine crests
and the dumb stones.

2

All the things
outside love
come to me now:
this landscape with its old man's understanding
begging to live
one more year, one more year,
one generation more,
one more eternity.

To bring forth thorns endlessly,
to rock dead stones
like children in their cradles
before they sleep.
To silence ancient memories,
one more one more
one more.

How strong the lust for life
in those about to die.
How terrible the longing
and how vain:
to live, to live
one more year, one more year,
one generation more,
one more eternity.

3

How could a joyous bird
lose itself in these hills?
With a love song in her throat,
her little heart throbbing with gladness,
the promise of young ones soon in the nest,
her wings hymning love.
But suddenly before her
from the blue height
unrolls
a wasteland
stoned to death.

Save her,
save her,
save her
from seeing
the corpse of every love,
the grave of every joy.

In her blue
altitudes
singing love,
solitary
she hangs,
without reaching
the death
that confronts her.

4

How can one bird alone
hold up the whole sky
over the waste
with fragile wings?
The sky is boundless and blue,
but it is uplifted by wings,
sustained by the song of a bird.

Thus did my heart sustain my love.
It was boundless and blue,
above all altitudes –
above wasteland
mounds of ruins
gulfs of grief.

Until the song in my breast grew silent,
its strength failed,
and turning to stone,
it fell.

My mute, wounded love –
how can one bird alone
hold up the whole sky?

From my mother's home

My mother's mother died
in the spring of her days. And her daughter
did not remember her face. Her portrait engraved
in my grandfather's heart
was struck from the world of images
after his death.

Only her mirror remains, sunk deeper with age
into its silver frame.
And I, her pale granddaughter, who do not resemble her,
peer into it today as if it were a pool
hiding its treasures
under the water.

Deep deep beyond my face
I see a young woman
pink-cheeked and smiling,
a wig on her head.
She is putting
a long earring into the lobe of her ear. Threading it
through a tiny hole in the delicate flesh.

Deep deep beyond my face
shines her eyes' bright gold.
The mirror carries on
the family tradition:
that she was beautiful.

A god once commanded us . . .

A god once commanded us to stand strong
under the terrible tree of life.
And in the black wind of the years we stood,
stricken with expectation –
perhaps the fruit would fall at our feet.
But nothing happened.

And on the day of secret reckoning
between him and us
we saw a hunched landscape, brown leaves falling,
and felt on our faces
a cold wind blowing.
Then said a Voice: this is your day of freedom.
This is everything. And this is good.

Now towards the flame of cutting cold, alone,
I take
a few steps only
until I meet
that flickering lantern
at the corner of the street.

Song of the Strange Woman

1

I am green and replete like a song that has blown
                                  through the grass,
I am deep and soft as a bird-nest,
I come from yesterday,
from the forest that taught me to breathe,
from the well where I drank of the light,
from the exhausted lovers embraced and sleeping
                                  in the grass.

I am from there,
from the village of the small winds,
from skies that weave low clouds with bluish smoke.
I hear your voices still,
blue as your smoke and dim.
I come from the village of clattering wooden spoons.
I am from there.

2

Windmill, windmill
over what shore did the gulls cry
the name of my dead land?
Windmill, windmill.

On what street did they walk
who did not turn their heads,
the kingdom of the sunset on their backs?
And the wings whirred in the wind.

Where?
Is the garden there, crimson
with fall, burying shadows,
hiding the twilights under the leaves,
making way, making way for the wind?

And the wind and the gull, did they cry
the name of my dead land?
Windmill, windmill!

3

Land of low clouds, I belonged to you.
I carry in my heart your every drop of rain.
On stumbling feet, without an angel to lean on, I
                                travel towards you,
bringing mushrooms of your forest to the kingdom
                                        of heaven.

In the kingdom of heaven, they still remember your
                                        feast day.
A gay harmonica is playing the song of the dead.
And a star entangled in the windmill's arms
is turning, turning –
and I have grown old, grown grey, and who will
                                dance with me?

Nevertheless, for the gate is open here,
I shall be at the festival:
I shall take off my shoes and sit down in the shade.
Slowly my face will float on a lazy stream,
my face lit up by the rivers
of your remembered shores.
Windmill, windmill!

Not for a long time now . . .

Not for a long time now has anyone waited for me.
Who will wait for a ship if there is no sea?
The circle draws in. Short is the way.
What's there to say?
Another year? Another month? Another day?

I shall lie under the earth, but something will remain above.
Somebody will hate somebody. Somebody will love.
The account is unsettled. Short is the way.
What's there to say?
Another year? Another month? Another day?

The dew falls and the evening chills my face.
At the street corner the same bus stops at the same place.
Tomorrow I shall wake again,
and again I shall say,
'Dear God!
Another year, another month, another day.'

That poem I didn't write . . .

That poem I didn't write
when I wrote poems –
I still remember everything about it,
every sound, every word.
But I shall not write it even now.

If I had written it then,
it would have been too naked a truth.
And if I wrote it today
it would be a total lie.

Come, descend to me, daughter of the gods,
nod your greying head
to me.

We shall play with words.

How lucid the world appears in this new game –

> not then, not now
> not false, not true

The two scales of the balance ascend and descend
in rhythm.

Heavenly Jerusalem, Jerusalem of the Earth

1

Divide your bread in two,
Heavenly Jerusalem, Jerusalem of the Earth,
jewels of thorn on your slopes
and your sun among the thistles.
A hundred deaths rather than your mercy!
Divide your bread in two,
one half for the birds of the sky:
the other,
for heavy feet to trample
at the crossroads.

2

People are walking in the counterfeit city
whose heavens passed like shadows,
and no one trembles.
Sloping lanes conceal
the greatness of her past.

The children of the poor
sing with indifferent voices:
'David, King of Israel, lives and is.'

3

Over my house
one late swallow.
All the other swallows
have already returned to the north.

Over my head
towards evening
in a city
weary of wanderings,
in a city of wanderers,
small, trembling wings
trace circles of despair.

A sky of Hebron glass.
The first lamp of night.
Swallow with no nest.
Arrested flight.

What now?

Toward Myself

The years have made up my face
with memories of love,
adorned my head
with silver threads
and made me beautiful.

Landscapes are reflected
in my eyes,
the paths I trod
have taught me to walk upright
with beautiful, though tired steps.

If you should see me now,
you would not recognise
the yesterdays you knew.
I go toward myself with a face
you looked for in vain
when I went toward you.

৵

GABRIEL PREIL

Night. And I am drinking . . .

1

Night. And I am drinking smoky black tea from China.
The cup is gay with flowers and figures of musicians.
Rice whitens in a saucer placid as a brook.
And from a pipe, tobacco
lures like dim gold.

My thoughts are folded now like birds on branches.
My feet rest, having trodden
the fields of obliteration.

2

I am a man approaching middle-age,
sitting by myself in the evening breeze of Brooklyn
as other men before me sat in their various Brooklyns,
making their calculations,

skulls furrowed, like mine, by wrinkles,
mouths, like mine, pain-twisted
for imagined or palpable reasons.

But he has still to come and fetch me,
descending from his mountain –
oblivion's dark master.

Words of oblivion and peace

TO JENNY N.

I once broke evening bread with the brown-faced, white-smiled
                                        Prince of Siam.
He wore festivity and humility as the first skin of his body.
His talk touched on London and New York – large villages
                                      lacking true wonders,
and his memory dwelt on the people of his country, small
                               of stature, eaters of pale rice,
and on the flowers there, high-tide huge, and summoning,
                            ablaze, the armies of their colours.
Lowering his low voice, 'There is nothing,' he said, 'like
                    the absolute oblivion that Buddha gives.
No small eddy will ever ruffle its seas,
and there is nothing like the calm of the endless seasons
                          that dream in its orchards.'

Suddenly, a wind blew from the corner of the street, a prayer
                      spoke from beyond the bridges,
but as the flesh grew sad and silent in its fated valleys,
through the window-pane there poured a peach and
                              northern sunset,
and I saw Jenny, the villages of her peaceful words in flower.

The Tired Hunter

Having written every kind of poem,
proud ones and shy ones,
weak ones and divinely wise ones,
your pen remains suspended
in the indifferent air,
even though the birds you once set flying
still sleep upon the cliffs,
and your colours
have not yet lost a sparkle of the kingdom.

Until you discover in the sharp light of noon
that the poems are only
blind arrows sent flying
to the heart of an imagined
eternal city
and you are only a hunter
who has at last grown tired.

The Eternal Present

My mother's uncle was physician to the Persian Shah.
Before this, or later, he built bridges near the Caspian Sea.
His greying photograph attests to his youth in 1888,
in Lithuania, close to the East Prussian border,
in the spring of a good wheat-year.

I don't know, however, the exact date of his sister's marriage,
but she gave birth to a daughter in the above-mentioned spring,
and she is, and has been for a long time now,
my mother – a baby-girl grown old.

And the summers and winters arrive in New York
year after year
and there is no then.
I am not a forgotten ring in a chain or a beloved heir.
I am a man engaged in talk this moment,
or biting into a pear, or drinking tea,
or listening behind the shutters
to the voice of the cantor on a Saturday night.

Here, of course, there is no mere historic documentary.
One present of dark and light exists.
There is no then.

A little research in snow

Snow, not the rare snow of Jerusalem,
but the casual New York kind
began to surround me
as candle after candle in me was lit,
each day a prophecy, each day a reward.
Even the weatherman
seemed notable for his kindness,
careful not to reveal
certain acidulous phenomena
somewhere invading a place, an ambiance.

I am a snowed-upon island now,
a single glint of a blade.
The possibilities for self-indulgence
have finally been sealed off.

From a late diary

Gabriel turned at last into old Mr Preil.
Overnight the pamperings began
that go with taking off a coat
and opening a door.
Suspicions and hypotheses
sprouted in him like weeds.

And he tried to ignore
the marginal in things,
the fortuity of time –
not wanting to give up
the wininess flowing in him,
and the streaming of his young streets.

As for the obtuse, they do not realise
that the self-same Gabriel
shares his time with them,
that no change threatens him.
It would also seem the coffee is hotter now,
and longer now the lightning-play of jets,
and longer lasting the bird-trees in full bloom.

A lesson in translation

FOR BETSY ROSENBERG

The translator tried to lay bare
the things that were not said,
the methods of design and indirection,
the compulsion to explore and to arrive,
once even reading something in my face.

More than anything she thought
to plough the unique subsoil,
to identify the bristle of roots,
the glow in the shaping.
There were moments when she was drawn by an image
like that of trees in the morning uttering birds,
or by the accidental – orchestrating of itself
a delicate irony, a yearning.

The original, we may assume, is still the original.
She did not make of it her own possession
or something other and different, though mine.
She kept, it seems, every stanza of the poem intact,
its credibility as usual flowing from autumn to autumn.

In spite of that, I question
how a cool and cautious text
can be turned into something sad, defeating peace.
Had I learned a lesson in translation?

A brief note from Jerusalem

The gentleman makes his way among clouds and moons,
saying to himself that he cannot learn a thing
even from the masters of nostalgia.
End of sentence.

As for the cypress, palm, and olive and their pretensions,
they are nothing more than wretched lab assistants.

Nevertheless, skies we call prophetic
seem to assail imported metaphors.
Street words are hurled about like kingly stones.
And a mountain-purple leaps with a strange, rock-like caress.
Somewhat confused, the gentleman begins
to fold up the map of what he had hoped to forget.

And now there was some respite from nostalgia.

Rain poem

Gabriel the rain-lover
sits in a cafe
thinking of the poem he's going to write,
if not today, tomorrow.

A poem, however, is not to be coerced
(if we may use slightly didactic language)
to come like tomorrows, like yesterdays,
arguing and bargaining
with a clock running down, a thermometer
                                    running wild.

It is a kind of extension of the rain
the-line-of-a-bird-or-plane
cutting through the black weather,
and it radiates some tentative reckoning
whose sum is an open question.

In any case, in a good poem
indifferences are flattened:
it is the history
of an exact line of tension,
of a garden
buffeted by hail.

With Walter and Amati

Dobbs Ferry in autumn. I with my pen
and Walter with his violins
that dangle like slabs of meat from hooks,
like ducks turning brown on spits,
or pears that ripen in their living gold.

Walter caresses his violins
as if he and they
were children deprived of caresses.
He passes a finger over the bow,
tries the quality of a string,
and listens deeply
as if in expectation of a word
that will be coming soon.

I too drift with a wave
to Cremona, city of violins,
and stop at Nicolo Amati's,
he who gave his instrument
the yellowish transparency
of a rare sunset hour,
or the darker tones
of an ordinary sunset at sea.

With some mysterious mixture
he glazed every flatness and rondure,
every concavity and convexity
of pine, maple, or willow
till the wood began of itself a music from within
even before the finished construct glowed.

GABRIEL PREIL   81

For all that, he did begin with material hardly poetic,
with potash, strange acids, flaxseed,
while from various directions
all kinds of coruscations passed over it in turn –
glowing towards burning gold and from it,
from reddish brown and towards it,
until they reached the blood hue of the mystical dragon,
so that I burn with the fire that lives in wood,
with the nightingale voice concealed in a violin string,
needing like them
the oxygen in air.

They are with Amati in Cremona,
I with Walter in Dobbs Ferry,
under the skies of autumn with my pen.

ZELDA

The crippled beggar . . .

The crippled beggar who lives
on the mad side of things
won't lean on the sun
any more –
dawn is a broken reed.
Won't lean on a leaf
any more –
spring is a broken reed.
Won't lean on the water
any more –
the river is a broken reed.
Won't lean on a swallow
any more –
the sky is a broken reed.
Won't lean on mankind
any more –
speech is a broken reed.
In darkness, decay, and death
God is his rest.
Only He
holds his hand.
The sun will not break
a vow of harmony
only to embrace

his howling heart.
The river won't flow
out of its circle of song
to extend a hand
to the outcast.

❦

YEHUDA AMICHAI

My father fought their war four years or so . . .

My father fought their war four years or so,
and did not hate or love his enemies.
Already he was forming me, I know,
daily, out of his tranquillities;

tranquillities, so few, which he had gleaned
between the bombs and smoke, for his son's sake,
and put into his ragged knapsack with
the leftovers of my mother's hardening cake.

He gathered with his eyes the nameless dead,
the many dead for my sake unforsaken,
so that I should not die like them in dread,
but love them, seeing them as once he saw.
He filled his eyes with them; he was mistaken.
Like them, I must go out to meet my war.

Savage memories

I think these days of the wind in your hair
and of my years in the world which preceded your coming,
and of the eternity to which I proceed before you;

and I think of the bullet that did not kill me,
but killed my friends –
they who were better than me because
they did not go on living;

and I think of you standing in summer
naked before the stove,
or bending, the better to read it, over a book
in the last light of day.

Yes, we had more than life.
We must now balance everything
with heavy dreams, and set
savage memories
upon what was once today.

All the generations before me

All the generations that preceded me contributed me
in small amounts, so that I would be erected here
                              in Jerusalem
all at once, like a house of prayer or a charity institution.
That commits one. My name is the name of my contributors.
That commits one.

I am getting to be the age my father was when he died.
My last will shows many superscriptions.
I must change my life and my death
daily, to fulfil all the predictions
concerning me. So they won't be lies.
That commits one.

I have passed my fortieth year.
There are posts they will not let me fill
because of that. Were I in Auschwitz,
they wouldn't put me to work.
They'd burn me right away.
That commits one.

What drove young Joseph . . .

What drove young Joseph to interpret dreams
must seal my lips.

What lulls the cradled child to sleep
keeps me awake, a fire.

What wounds and storms and opens an oak to fall
closes me like a fist.

The gate that opens to your realms of day
seals, like a valve, my way.

The thoughts came to him . . .

The thoughts came to him like long lines of freight,
a convoy of supplies before the battle.
They came to him in order, one by one,
and while he was unloading them, he thought

them out in sentences, in neat array.
The shots were commas, full stops, dots above
the i's. The earth exploded just when he
had brought me to the surface of his love.

And in the spring, he felt his fingers tingle,
like branches of a tree, with blossoming,
and he prepared for fruit. But in the fall,

twice wounded in his legs, twisting, he fell
to earth; like Balaam, falling, could foretell
the story of my days, and sang the blessing.

A pity. We were such a good invention

They amputated
your hips from my loins.
For my part, they will always be
surgeons. All of them.

They dismantled us
each from each.
For my part, they are engineers.
All of them.

We were a good, a loving
invention: a plane made from a man and woman,
wings and all.
We rose a little from the earth.
We flew a little.

Half of the people in the world . . .

Half of the people in the world
love the other half;
half of the people
hate the other half.
Must I, because of these and those,
forever change
like rain in all its seasons? Sleep among the rocks,
grow rough as olive bark
and listen to the moon howl over me?

Must I with worry camouflage my love,
grow like grass, fearful between the tracks,
live like a mole in earth,
with roots and not with branches,
and not with angels cheek to cheek?
Must I snatch love in the first cave;
marry my girl
under the canopy whose posts hold up the earth;
act out my death, always
to the last breath and the last
word and without understanding?
And build my house – flagpoles above,
bomb shelter below – and then go forth on roads
made only for returning? Must I undergo
the terrible stations:
cat, stick, fire, water and slaughter,
between the kid and the angel of death?
Half of the people love;
half, hate.
And where shall I find my place between these
halves who suit each other so?
Through what crack shall I see
the white dwellings of my dreams,
the barefoot runners on the sands;
or see, at least, the waving handkerchief
of a girl beside the hill?

Lips of the dead once thoughtlessly . . .

Lips of the dead once thoughtlessly
whispered a single word in earth;
exaggerating now, each tree
has overdone its springtime birth.

Earth rips her bandages again.
She wants no healing. She wants pain.
Spring is not peace; it is not rest;
spring is enemy terrain.

If anyone could reach that goal,
young lovers could in one patrol;
forth we were sent to Rainbow Land;

although we knew: the dead return;
although we knew: the storm is born
out of a young girl's open hand.

YEHUDA AMICHAI

The two of us together, each of us alone

('Jointly and severally' – from a lease contract)

Summer, my dearest, turns again to the dark,
and the lights are all out in the old Fun Park.
The see-saws still go up and down.
The two of us together, each of us alone.

Empty the sea where her ships used to go.
Hard to hold on to anything now.
The soldiers once waited behind the hill.
How much we need of mercy still.
The two of us together, each of us alone.

The moon is sawing the clouds in two.
Let us make love with the armies in view.
Between the armed camps, our parleying
may still perhaps change everything.
The two of us together, each of us alone.

As the first sweet rain was once salt sea,
so, it seems, has my love changed me.
I fall to you slowly. Receive me, love.
No angel saves us from above.
For the two of us are together. Each of us is alone.

The death of my father

From all the rooms, my father suddenly
departed for strange distances, for he

had gone to call on God somehow
so He would come to our assistance now.

And God took up the burden and came soon,
hanging His jacket on the hook of moon,

though He will never let our father go
who went to fetch His help for us below.

Couplets

1

If once again a flood fell from the spheres,
we would be on the Ark with all the pairs.

Both with the adder and the elephant,
with the defiled and with the innocent.

Noah would keep us wrapped, like vine shoots curled,
for a new planting in a better world.

2

Like the stone arch of ancient windows, we
from the ledge will rise in singularity;

rising together and facing each,
one leans on other, thus to mend the breach.

Till brought together at the keystone crown,
we shall find rest – our forehead one.

Always we shall see flowers on the sill,
and always the roads, if we look farther still.

3

Above, pine cones and birds upon the bough.
Bird song and dream within the heart, below.

Our stranded shoes, whose open mouths gape air,
behold the heavens, too. The thoroughfare

almost arrived here, but considering
the short eternity these lovers, murmuring,

found here, not distant from their daily lives,
went roundabout and left them to themselves.

Not like the cypress

Not like the cypress,
not all at once, not all of me,
but like the grass,
with thousands of green, of careful arrivals;
like children in that game where many hide
and one goes looking.

Not like an only son,
like Saul, the son of Kish, whom the many found
and made into a king.
But like the rain in many places,
from many clouds: to seep through, to be drunk
by many mouths; breathed
like the air all year and sprinkled wide
like a spring flower.

Not the shrill ring which wakes
the doctor on duty at the clinic gate,
but with a knocking at side entrances,
at many obscure doors, with many knockings
                                    of the heart.

And afterwards, the silent exodus: like smoke
without fanfare, resigning ministers,
children grown tired of their games;
or like a stone, beyond steep slopes,
in its last rolling, in that place where begins
the plain of the great renunciation,
from which like prayers,
a cloud of motes, the dust arises.

Don't prepare for tomorrow . . .

Don't prepare for tomorrow, enter the narrow lane,
intend the dream. Steps will lead you. Bury your plans
like spilt blood in the sand. And break your journey
before you come to the sharp turning,
which in any case will break it.

Return what has been lent your body – return your blood.
It will not stray. Water will change to flowers,
wine evaporate, the way life leaves a man
at a pounding on the door. Don't open. Stay
inside. Sit in the dark. Stand
where the murmur of those who pray is like the murmur
of sea-waves. And don't try to ask, What is it?
This is the place. Don't move.
You have made your way.
You have wept. You have smiled.
Your photo has been snapped.

Look at the girls jumping rope. The destiny of a rope
hit by the ground and rising like a gate above them.
Don't interrupt now. Stand on the side.
Turn, go, buy yourself
a slave in the wind. And like a swimmer,
push the world aside with arms and legs. This
will hit the face of the water and hurt it, but will leave you
still above, still among the living. Don't cut yourself off,
but weep your future
into a lap. Sit for a long while
before a woman. Don't speak. That, too, is prophecy.
And on a slope, love the stone placed like you
beneath the wheel to stop time rolling.

Don't strike the names of the dead
from the name-plates in the doorways. What if they don't
live here any more. What if their names
are already carved on tombstones.
Their names will be double: there and here.
And those slowly-closing, there terrible doors,
don't let them
close upon you. Interpose, no matter what,
between the doorpost and the door:
a shoe, your hand, last words. This will hurt,
but this will keep you going.
Examine your new feelings, outside,
as you would new weapons
far from the last houses
in a hidden valley, early, at absolute dawn.

And be like your mother on a Sabbath eve
screening herself from her candles.
Afterwards, like her, remove the concealing hands
and bless, but only if you know that everything remains
and is really yours.
Then say the blessing.

❦

DAN PAGIS

Autobiography

I died with the first blow and was buried
in the stony field.
The raven showed my parents
what to do.

If my family is famous, not a little of the credit
goes to me.
My brother invented murder,
my parents – crying.
I invented silence.

Afterwards, those well-known events took place.
Our inventions were perfected.
One thing led to another,
call-up notices went out
and there were those who killed in their own way,
cried in their own way.

Out of consideration for the reader,
I am not naming names.
At first, the details horrify;
in the end, they bore.

You can die once, twice, even seven times,
but you cannot die a thousand times.
I can.
My underground cells reach everywhere.

When Cain started to multiply on the face of the earth,
I started to multiply in the belly of the earth.
For a long time now, my strength has been greater
than his.
His legions desert and go over to me.
And even this is only half a revenge.

The battle

With huge, with strangers' eyes,
with shattered brow,
the dead gather, stupid with surprise,
at the mouth of pits. Slow
over terror's border come
columns and columns, struck dumb,
mouths gaping wide. None can know
who the curst are, who the blest
in the burnt dust.

Evidence

No. No. They were certainly
human beings. Uniforms, boots.
How to explain? They were created
in the Image.

I, too, in the Image.
But I had a different creator.

And He in His goodness
left nothing in me that could die.
I fled towards Him,
rising weightless, bluish, reconciled –
apologetic, even:
smoke rising to omnipotent smoke
that has no body or form.

Roll-call

He stands, cold in the morning wind,
stamping his feet, rubbing his hands,
death's diligent angel
who worked hard and rose in rank.
Suddenly he feels he has made a mistake. All eyes,
he checks again in his open book
the bodies waiting for him in formation,
a square within a circle. Only I
am missing. I am a mistake.
I extinguish my eyes quickly; erase my shadow.
Please God, let me not be missed, let the sum
add up without me.

Ready

Like all the apes in the neighborhood,
I, too, grow bitter as I swing from branch to branch:
the past age that was full of sun has passed.
It's cold now. The nuts have become too hard.
The beasts of prey grow more and more cunning.
I've had it. I'm leaving. Goodbye.

What's happening?
My tongue twists in my mouth.
My shoulders – where are my shoulders going? –
suddenly straightening,
pushing back firmly.
Suddenly I have forced upon me –
what? – a high forehead!

This quiet is good. I'm almost, almost perfected.
I choose for myself a nice suit,
button it, zip it, light up a cigarette slowly,
and sit down at the table with my stop-watch,
the one friend I possess,
completely ready
for the invention of chess.

The Mosquito

Legend has it that the Emperor Titus was
punished for destroying the Temple in
Jerusalem by having a mosquito buzz in
his ear day and night.

The mosquito lives
in Titus' left ear,
a tiny electric drill
that pierces the screaming emperor
like wax.

The labyrinth's inner coils
do not confuse him,
do not seduce him at all.
His is a hidden task: to find
the shortest route
leading to the treasure.

Balloons

Party balloons rub against each other
among the paper serpents,
and timidly accept their limits, the ceiling.
They heed all hints,
meekly respond to the least gust.
But even for these gentle creatures
the last hour must come.
Suddenly their souls escape

with a fearful whistle,
or bust
with a pop.
Afterward, the rubber corpses decay
on the fringes of a filthy mat,
and their souls stray
seeking repose
in the floating middle-world
at the level of the nose.

The late author: snapshot in the rain

And so, Ernie, your laughing head floats
between the black arches
in the cathedral of an open umbrella.
I read your wrinkles and grow terrified.
Fabricator, fabricator. How did you guess me
before I was?

Your moustache mocks. Having compromised
                                   between two ends.
You are a monk who fled in a shabby robe
from the common sense of oblong Manhattan.
You are an unbeliever, Ernie. The rain prays
for your seven souls.

What you never doubted was this finger of yours.
It grew with you,
typed your books.
In the end, it pressed the trigger
and beckoned: Come. All is as you expected.

Ein Leben

The month she died,
she is standing at her window,
a young woman with an elegant permanent
in a brown photograph
pensively looking outside.

Outside, an afternoon cloud of 1924
is gazing at her – blurred, unfocused,
but faithful to her forever. Inside,
the someone looking at her is me,
almost four years old,

stopping my ball in air,
slowly stepping out of the photograph
and growing old, growing old
carefully, quietly
so as not to startle her.

Winter's end

Good snowman,
your coal eyes envision blackness,
only blackness. How much courage
is reflected in your eyes.
Not a single blink. In the centre,
your nose still protrudes a little,
that pessimistic carrot.
Rejoice, my friend, in your old age.
It's true that you and I at winter's end
are somewhat less substantial than we were,
but you know, just as well as I,
your winter days like mine were beautiful,
and beautiful will be our summer.
Why are we waiting for it in the back yard?
Let us steal away from here right now
before the spring mud, and course
swiftly and light-heartedly
down the sloping road and onward
toward the wide sea – if it really exists.
Tomorrow the radio will announce
that no trace of us
will ever be found.

NATAN ZACH

Seven

I, who was lower than any worm,
read Brenner, *Steppenwolf* and Vogel.
I studied literature, wrote poems. Experiments.
I didn't want to limit myself.
I had all sorts of plans. Including travel.
In the meanwhile I crammed for tests. Girls helped
to pass the time. I listened to music, now
under the ground.

I owned a garage, thank God.
I had – and I'll make it short – a house, a car, trips to Europe,
Children – as one should – friends, evenings of bridge,
excursions to the sea. Suddenly
I was called up. I didn't know a damned thing.
Nobody did. I am not a politician. I didn't get around
to arranging for insurance. It's still impossible to be sure
about anything now under the ground.

I was completely against. Not that I
justify them, but I don't justify ourselves either
one hundred per cent. There are no saints in this business.
The politicians and the journalists are to blame. On
                                        both sides.

Something ought to have been done, like working out a
                                        policy, drawing maps,
advising the return of all the territories except Jerusalem.
The religious, in any case, I don't like. You can say that
                                        I even hate them
now under the ground.

I'm still pretty new here. Not an old-timer. Transylvania.
Everyone complains. Not me. A joy I have.
A family I have. So what's there to complain about?
Of course it's not all peaches and cream. But is America
                                        any better?
Let others go to America. I don't need millions. Only
enough to live on. When I come home,
I play a little with the children, eat well,
look at television. On Saturdays we go to the sea.
No car. So what? I live near the sea.
So what do they have to complain about
now under the ground?

I died a natural death. I am a woman.
Me – nothing ever happened to me. My husband died
twenty years ago. I went on living. I didn't
have children. I didn't remarry. You don't have to marry
just to be married if you don't meet the right man.
I was always so careful. Here people drive like mad.
I simply crossed the street, and funny thing is that I did look.
But I don't know. I got confused
now under the ground.

I still don't know how it happened. I was forty-six.
I should have been transferred already to the civil guard.
                                        They promised.

It couldn't go on like this: called up for a month each time.

And every year.

The papers should have come. When I heard the sirens
I didn't suspect a thing. Who could have suspected
a thing like that? Especially
when the papers were supposed to come at any time.
In my unit I was already down for transfer
to another unit
now under the ground.

Listen, pal – I used to say – a man who goes to one war
is a patriot. A man who goes to two – is unlucky.
But a man who goes to three is just a damned fool.
That's rich. Ain't it? You don't have to take things too much
to heart. What good does that do? Life is a game.
The world is a stage. That's what I always used to say.
But he got on my nerves, that lieutenant-colonel. No sense

of humour.

More brains in his little finger than in his whole head.
That's rich, ain't it? But it'll pass, like everything else. Just

take it easy.

For this you don't have to go and kill yourself
now under the ground

*   *   *

We are seven
buried on a hill
near the town.
No sheep will crop the grass on our graves,
no thorn pierce the flesh.
Life goes on, as they say. And ends.
We were, as they say, a door

to the wide world, truly a spacious world.
We could walk, beget, suffer.
We were a corridor
leading nowhere.
We realise that today.
They will remember us – those who can't forget.
Our image fades moment by moment.
We are seven
buried on a hill
near the town.

Failure

'Stop,' cried the wolf to the lamb seven
times. It was only then that he ate him.

What compels me to be drawn
to whatever the heart is drawn to?

What makes me try to part
the indivisible –

water from water? Changed to air
only in heaven.

The heart meanwhile remains
fragile

as ever –
everything

that never rose to the bait
dangling on its hook.

DAVID AVIDAN

Six local poems

1
A man takes off . . .

Before a man goes to sleep a man takes off
his pants and hangs them on a chair
arranges for the phone to wake him up
goes to the john i.e. the privy
i.e. the toilet i.e. the WC
before a man goes to sleep a man takes off his clothes
inspects his body in a glass and goes to sleep
with a space-pilot worry-flicker in his eye
instructions for improving the landing improving
                                        the language
at that hour when one is landing and falling asleep

2

A man hangs up . . .

A man hangs up his pants and plans his virility
hangs his pants on a chair and determines a stance
determines a stance re further verse and makes an advance
makes an advance and casts a glance at the glass and
                                                  makes a movie
makes a movie and hangs up his pants and plans

determines a stance re further plans and lowers
then raises a glance at the glass and makes a movie
a man puts on his pants and begins to manage his plant
so many yards from the start of his stores to the end of his fly

to where his debts end and his income begins
a man wears out his pants and extends the stretch of his land
east and west north and south to no matter what shore
still in range of the sixth and the red fleet's men-of-war

3

When a man . . .

When a man gets up in the early hours of day
he puts on his pants and starts shooting right away
at bed and balcony at books and looking-glass
and water running after him in a mass.
A man gets up at dawn and before you can say
cock robin puts on his pants and drowsily shoots away

DAVID AVIDAN   111

4

A man hangs on . . .

A man returns to a flat and hangs on to a machine
hangs on to a typing machine at a time not timely
a hand hangs on to a typing machine a man puts off his sleep
how many seconds hours years will he stay awake
a man wakes up a typing machine and hangs on to his sleep
a man returns to his flat and puts his machine to work
the machine that more or less is really the right machine
he puts his waking machine to work and puts off his sleep
how many seconds hours years will he stay awake
in this flat in this land no matter where he may be
still in range of the American or the Russian navy.

5

Summation

Before a man
a man hangs
when a man gets up
a man hangs on

6
Tax-free supplement for diplomatic expenses

Two words on the problematic status of erection
against a backdrop of subsiding class-struggle
and the stiffening stands of the great powers:
it is clear, for instance, that every substantial stiffening
is increasingly appreciable in the face of a softening,
some degree of softening, a measurable softening
of the opposing side, which, by the way,
seldom gets soft enough
to enable a really stiff position to come to full expression
with secure and agreed-on borders, with a minimum
                              shedding of speeches.
And the God of Hosts will have mercy on all his Jews,
and Allah on all his Muslims
and God-of-Hosts-Israel-and-God-of-Hosts-Allah
will empty words and shells
all day and all night.
These are the main points
listed checked delivered
for a peace offensive
initiated
when the day comes
after the war.

Life of a dead dog

A lonely man – leads a dog's life.
A dog – leads a lonely man's life.
Out of great loneliness I bought myself a dog.
Since then my life has been filled with barking:

> How, how,
> How do you do, sir?
> How do, do, do,
> Do, do, do, do –
> How?

The dog was small and then.
In time he grew big and fat.
In time he learned how to talk,
And now he asked the first thing every morning:

> How, how, etc.

The dog was big and fat.
In time he learned how to bite.
In time he gained self-assurance.
And now he asked the first thing every morning:

> How, how, etc.

The dog was big and a biter,
but he had no one to bite.
Me it was loneliness bit, night after night,
and now he asked the first thing every morning:

> How, how, etc.

Loneliness bit me night after night
till a woman entered my life.
The dog was fat and a biter –
so he bit her in his rage:

>How, how,
>How do you do, ma'am?
>How do, do, do,
>Do, do, do, do –
>How?

I drew my army revolver
and aimed it straight at his head.
Calmly I squeezed the trigger
and forced myself not to weep:

>Boom! Boom!
>Dy, dooh, dah, dooh, dy
>Dy, dooh, dooh, dy
>Dy, dooh, dooh, dy
>Boom! Die!

A man who loves doesn't lead a dog's life.
A dog dies – when a man loves.
Out of great love I killed me a dog.
Since then there has been no barking in my life:

>How, how,
>How did I do it,
>How did, did, did,
>Did, did, did, did –
>Dead.

All the choruses except the sixth were originally written in English by the poet.

❦

DALIA RAVIKOVITCH

Clockwork Doll

I was a clockwork doll that night,
and I turned left and I turned right,
and when I fell and broke to bits,
they recomposed my wax and wits.

I was a proper doll once more,
my manner carefully demure;
and yet a doll of another kind –
an injured twig that tendrils bind.

And when they asked me to a ball –
although my steps were rhythmical,
they partnered me with dog and cat.

My hair was gold, my eyes were blue.
I wore a dress where flowers grew.
Cherries blazed on my straw hat.

DALIA HERTZ

The return

I returned with a bottle of wine, with a deck of cards,
                                        with flowers.
I pressed the electric button. Pressed the elevator button.
                                        Rang the door bell.
My hands that had rested in the air and dangled gracefully,
                deprived of excitement like an expert angel,
touched actually my heart, which always in moments
                                like these, completely
leaves me, surrounds me, warms me, gives me cover,
steals my excitement and inherits it – and there it is,
                                        natural, red
and provocative. But enough of these terrible comparisons.
The mother opened the door. The father opened the door.
                The brother and the sister. All of them,
all of them opened the door, and an old song began,
                                the melody sang itself.
I presented them with the wine and with the flowers.
                                        Behind me,
the light on the stairs went out. Before me,
the hall light seemed to long for my body.
Caged corners in the living-room, drawers embedded in
                the walls, called to parts of my body

to come and sit down, to come and see, to come and
                                   get warm.
And we played poker. I lost, on purpose, every cent I had.
                          And I didn't diddle anyone.
I had another bite to eat. I touched my father gently.
                          Gently touched my mother.
I didn't go outside, didn't abandon the pantry – not the
                          shelves, not the towels.
It seemed to me that every wall was a new mattress on
                          which I could sleep,
every bed an old wall on which I could lean,
and it is up to me to prolong this visit
although my words about it are about to end.

❧

ZALI GUREVITCH

Everyone's dancing where I live . . .

Everyone's dancing where I live
although one dancer thought that if
one dancer should be missing, then
he could never dance again

Sitting all the dances out
he soon was followed by the rout
who one by one emptied the hall
the dancers now are sitting all

and all are sitting where I live
although one dancer thought that if
he danced alone, a private whim,
everyone would bow to him

And so he danced his dance. The crowd
stood up as one and to him bowed
and then a second joined the dance
and all the others now advance

Now all are dancing where I live
now all are sitting where I live
now all are thinking where I live

Line of a poem

The segmented line
is like walking,
which turns itself into a road

each foot
step coming to its end
in an enormous
a terrifying meadow

What is wiser than the path
that leads the beast to a waterhole
each evening

Biographical notes

Haim Nachman Bialik (1873–1934) was born in the Ukrainian village of Radi and settled in Tel Aviv in 1924. He began publishing in the 1890s, after moving to Odessa and coming under the influence of its Jewish literary circles, and was rapidly hailed as the leading poet of the Hebrew national revival movement. In addition to writing, prophet-like, verse of wrath in response to the Russian progroms of 1903–6, Bialik wrote poems of great lyric intensity, infused with longing and despair. The poet's fine tonal modulations and natural cadences (adopted from Russian accentual-syllabic meter), breathing into Hebrew a 'new song', are sharply counterpointed by Bialik's lonely, brooding voice, speaking, as it were, in the wake of national and personal ruin. Though writing very little verse after 1911, Bialik remained active in the public sphere. He founded Dvir publishing house, edited and published works of the Hebrew medieval poets, published short stories and literary essays and compiled (with Y. H. Ravnitzky) an important anthology of rabbinic lore.

Yaakov Fichman (1880–1958) was born in Bessarabia and like many writers of his generation wandered in Europe (Warsaw, Kishinev, Vilna, Odessa, Berlin) before settling in Palestine in 1925. Poet, critic, essayist and translator into Hebrew of Heine and Goethe, Fichman wrote finely wrought lyrical–impressionistic verse with a keen eye for the landscapes of both Europe and Palestine.

Yaakov Steinberg (1887–1947) was born in the Ukraine and after residencies in Odessa, Warsaw, Kiev and Switzerland settled in

Palestine in 1914. Translator, short-story writer, and a highly original essayist, Steinberg wrote a poetry characterised by its anti-romantic, at times decadent atmosphere. He is the most Baudelarian of the early Hebrew moderns in his tightly crafted lyric statements of urban world-weariness and unfulfilled desires.

Rachel (1890–1931) was born in Viatka in Russia and in 1909 settled in Palestine. There she worked as a farm labourer, first in Rehovot and later in the vicinity of the Kinneret. Between 1913 and 1919, she studied agriculture in France and Russia. Rachel spent several years as a member of Kibbutz Degania, but had to leave when she was found to be suffering from consumption, of which she eventually died. Her delicate, short lyrics, written in the cadences of spoken Hebrew, have remained immensely popular, and many of her poems have been set to music.

David Vogel (1891–1943?) was born in Podolia, Russia. He lived in Vienna between 1911 and 1925, spent two years in Palestine, and then moved to Berlin and, finally, to Paris. He was captured by the Nazis in 1943 and sent to a concentration camp where he perished. In addition to poetry, Vogel published short stories, a novella, and a major novel, *Married Life*. As with Avraham Ben Yitzhak, Vogel's subtle, irregular rhythms and highly personal, expressionistic tone (markedly influenced by the poetry of Rilke and Trakl) made his work a model for a new generation of Israeli poets writing in the fifties.

Uri Zvi Greenberg (1894–1981) was born in Galicia and, after serving in the Austro-Hungarian army during World War I, settled in Palestine in 1924. That same year he joined the Revisionist movement and became its leading intellectual spokesman. Subsequently, he spent a number of years in Warsaw as editor of the Revisionist weekly *Die Welt*, but with the outbreak of World War II, he escaped from Poland and returned to Palestine. Greenberg's early work was written in Yiddish. His first book of Hebrew verse was published in 1928. His Whitmanesque, hortatory poetry is forceful, rich in expression and intensely Jewish-messianic in its themes.

Esther Raab (1894–1981) was born in Palestine. She attended a teachers' training college, worked both as a farmer and a teacher, and lived in Cairo for four years in the 1920s. More than any other poet of her generation, she seizes in her poems upon the particulars of her native landscape. Shunning broad, communal themes, her poetry adapts its rhythms to the harsh, irregular contours of the land.

Yocheved Bat-Miriam (1901–79) was born in Russia and attended universities in Odessa and Moscow before settling in Palestine in 1926. Like her contemporaries, Leah Goldberg and Natan Alterman, Bat-Miriam assimilated the techniques of the Russian symbolists and poets influenced by them, including Boris Pasternak. She wrote with a keen sense of place – both of her childhood home and Palestine. Although adhering to strict metrical form, her use of language is idiosyncratic and daring in its syntax, with frequent metaphorical leaps. Bat-Miriam wrote no poetry after 1948, the year of her son's death in the War of Independence.

Hayim Lenski (1905–42?) was born in White Russia and eventually settled in St Petersburg. In 1934 he was arrested for writing Hebrew and was sentenced to five years hard labour in Siberia. He continued to write Hebrew poems while in the camps and his poems continued to reach Palestine until 1937, when the flow stopped. Lenski returned to St Petersburg after having served his time, but within a short time he was arrested again and sent to Siberia, where he died of hunger. In 1958 a manuscript by Lenski containing a hundred and thirty-one unpublished poems reached Israel. Lenski wrote sonnets, ballads and satires in a sonorous Hebrew enriched by startling imagery. It is a poetry of private concerns, of childhood memories and – particularly in the later work – of the hardship of forced labour and imprisonment.

Natan Alterman (1910–70) was born in Warsaw and settled in Tel Aviv in 1925. He studied agronomy in Nancy, but eventually took up a journalistic post. Markedly influenced by Russian and French symbolism, Alterman rapidly established himself as the leading poet and polemicist of the forties and fifties. He wrote descriptive, symbolist lyrics using a wide range of traditional forms, and also published topical verse under the heading 'The Seventh Column'. The latter played a critical role in expressing and shaping public opinion in the early days of Israeli statehood. Alterman was also known for his outstanding translations of Shakespeare, Racine and Molière.

Leah Goldberg (1911–70) was born in Koenigsberg (now Kaliningrad) and spent her early years in Kovno (now Kaunas), Lithuania. She emigrated to Palestine in 1935, after receiving her PhD in Semitic languages at the University of Bonn. Her pared-down style is deceptively simple, even when using traditional forms, such as the sonnet sequence. She was associated with the Hebrew modernist movement, led by Avraham Shlonsky, and with him edited an influential anthology of Russian poetry in translation. She also translated from the English, Italian, French, Greek and Russian. Her translations of *As You Like It* and of Petrarch's sonnets are considered modern Hebrew classics. She taught from 1952 till the end of her life in the Department of Comparative Literature at the Hebrew University, Jerusalem.

Gabriel Preil (1911–93) was born in Estonia and went to live in the United States in 1922. He started writing in Yiddish but switched to Hebrew in the 1930s, gradually adopting to Hebrew the supple, conversational rhythms of such American poets as Robert Frost and William Carlos Williams. By the 1940s Preil's poems were being published regularly in Israeli periodicals and he was hailed as an important influence on the younger generation of Israeli poets who were turning away from Russian and French symbolism and reading, for the first time, the English and American poets. Preil died while on a visit to Jerusalem, awaiting the publication of his *Collected Poems*.

Zelda (1914–84), née Mishkovsky, was born in Chernigov, in the Ukraine, and emigrated to Palestine in 1925. She lived in Mea Shearim, the ultra-Orthodox neighbourhood of Jerusalem, and taught in Orthodox schools for girls. Her first collection, fusing deep religious feeling and often startling imagery with clear, unadorned diction, was published in 1967 and won her immediate critical and popular acclaim.

Yehuda Amichai (b.1924) was born in Germany and moved to Jerusalem with his family in 1936. He served with the Jewish Brigade in World War II and as an infantryman in the War of Independence. Amichai is Israel's most lauded and popular contemporary poet. Rich in imagery, the poetry deftly applies the rhythms and idioms of daily speech and blends the commonplace with the sacral. His poetry has been extensively translated and he has given numerous readings abroad. Amichai is also the author of a collection of short stories and a novel.

Dan Pagis (1930–86) was born in Radautz, Bukovina. Interned during World War II in a Ukrainian concentration camp, he escaped in 1944 and two years later came to Israel. Pagis taught at the Hebrew University and was a leading scholar of medieval Hebrew poetry. His is a poetry of wit, detachment and near surgical control. Though elegant and even colloquial in tone, Pagis wrote primarily as a survivor of the Holocaust, from the nether side of the living, in the voice of the disembodied.

Natan Zach (b.1930) was born in Berlin and settled in Palestine with his family in 1935. Poet and critic, Zach took a leading role in the reformulation of a new Hebrew poetics in the late fifties and early sixties. His own poetry, subtle, disengaged, ironic and musically evocative, had a tremendous impact on young writers and the general public. Zach has translated plays by Frisch, Brecht and Dürrenmatt, as well as Palestinian Arab folk-poetry (in collaboration with Rashed Hussein).

David Avidan (1934–95) was born in Tel Aviv. Gadfly and *provocateur* of the Israeli literary scene, Avidan in his poetry was playful, self-mocking, and – in sharp contrast to his elders – garrulous. His formally diverse, highly inventive work is reminiscent of Frank O'Hara's virtuoso urban chatter. The all-inclusive and expansive dimension of his poetry had a marked influence on the new wave of poets who began publishing in the late sixties and early seventies.

Dalia Ravikovitch (b.1936) was born in Ramat Gan and studied at the Hebrew University. She published her first collection of poems while in the army and was immediately recognised as a leading new voice, at once disenchanted, restrained and delicately sensual. In recent years her poetry has become more engaged, particularly in its treatment of the Israeli–Palestinian conflict as seen from a woman's perspective.

Dalia Hertz was born in Tel Aviv and studied philosophy at Tel Aviv University, as well as at Oxford. Her hard-edged poems speak for a new generation growing up in modern-day Tel Aviv and, alongside such poets as Yona Wollach and Meir Wieseltier, she was associated in the late sixties with the new avant-guarde. For ten years she edited the weekly Israeli Radio literary magazine.

Zali Gurevitch (b.1949) grew up in a suburb of Tel Aviv and studied at the Hebrew University, where he currently lectures in the department of sociology. He has, since the mid-seventies, published six volumes of poetry, essays on contemporary Hebrew poetry and painting and a volume of translations of the poetry of John Ashbery.

Gabriel Levin (b.1948) was born in Paris and has lived in Jerusalem since 1972. He has published two books of poetry, most recently *Ostraca*, Anvil Press, 1999.

Robert Friend was born in Brooklyn in 1913. He settled in Israel in 1950 and taught English and American literature at the Hebrew University in Jerusalem for more than thirty years. He published eight books of poetry, the last one being *The Next Room*, Menard Press, 1995. He also published four books of poetry translations, including *Flowers of Perhaps: Selected Poems of Ra'hel*, Menard Press, 1994. He died in Jerusalem in 1998.